A Rapid Rescue

Tony Bradman ● Jonatronix

OXFORD

UNIVERSITY PRESS

CODE Control Update:

My name is **CODE**. I am the computer that controls **Micro World**. **Team X** and **Mini** are trying to get the **CODE keys** and rescue **Macro Marvel**. My **BITEs** must stop them!

Team X are in: Fiendish Falls zone

Team X

Mini

CODE key

BITE

2

Fiendish Falls cameras

A swoopie grabbed Ant and took him to its nest.

Hippos capsized Cat and Tiger's boat.

The Croco-BITE attacked Cat and Tiger.

They hung on to creepers to escape.

Status: Max, Ant, Mini and Rex are still looking for the BITE.

Before you read

Sound checker
Say the sounds.

ie　s　tch　ture

Tricky words
called
friend

Sound spotter
Blend the sounds.

sh	r	ie	k	ed

t	r	ea	s	ure

s	t	r	e	tch	ed

a	d	v	e	n	ture

Into the zone

Do you have something that you really treasure?
What would you do if you lost it?

4

"I'm going to find out about the BITE on my Gizmo," Mini told Ant. Suddenly, Max's boat bumped into their boat. Ant and Mini tried to steady themselves, but Mini felt herself wobble.

splash!

"I don't believe it!" Mini shrieked.
"I've dropped my Gizmo!"

"I'm going to treasure my Gizmo from now on," said Mini.
Ant sighed. "What an adventure!"

Now you have read ...
A Rapid Rescue

Take a closer look

Mini dropped the Gizmo into the water.

How do you think Mini **felt** when she dropped the Gizmo?

What did she **say**?

What was she **thinking**?

Thinking time

Explain how Mini, Ant and Max used these items to help them save the Gizmo.

X-ray glasses	Green Dart	rope

Ant looked into the swampy water. He spied the Gizmo, but it was being carried away by the current.

Max and Rex's boat was floating
away, but Max had a plan.
He shared it with his friends.
"Catch this!" Max called.

8

To the falls

It was the Green Dart!

9

Ant shrank and got inside the Green Dart. He chased the Gizmo and quickly captured it.

Ant had the Gizmo, but the current was strong. Both Ant and Mini were being swept towards the Fiendish Falls!

They were getting closer and closer to the giant waterfall.
It was down to Mini to save them both.
She grabbed a rope that was by her feet.

Mini measured out a huge loop of rope and threw it over a rock on the nearest island.

The rope held Mini's boat still. She stretched out and snatched the Green Dart just in time.